The Psalms
as Israel's Prayer
and Our Own

Christian Heritage Rediscovered

The Series, as the name suggests, is meant to focus on Christian Faith & Living vis-à-vis topics like Literature & Poetry, Indigenous Philosophizing, Ethical response towards Agriculture, Health & Healing, Science & Technology, Ecofeminist Theology, Sociological approach towards Human Rights, Law & Politics, Arts, History of Ideas, Ancient Civilizations, Cultural Contiguity, Religious Cosmologies & Mysticism, Footsteps of famous Theologians, World Peace & Harmony, Global Capitalism, Network Marketing, Cybertheology, Population & Demographics, Epigraphic Studies, Contextualized Education, and many others. We welcome a Mss. on any topic/s mentioned, whether they are original works, scholarly monographs, collections of conference papers, revised dissertations, or translations of historical documents. Through the Series we, the Publishers, are striving to put forward published works that may help Institutions, Academic Bodies, Researchers, Scholars and the World at large in furthering their respective knowledge and understanding on the concerned subject. We welcome your comments on our efforts and further suggestions on how we can foster the upcoming thoughtful theologically grounded books.

The Psalms as Israel's Prayer and Our Own

Dr. Robert D. Miller II, OFS
Associate Professor of Old Testament
Catholic University of America

Christian World Imprints™

© Robert D. Miller II

First Published in 2013 by

Christian World Imprints™
Christian Publishing & Books from India
H-12 Bali Nagar, **New Delhi-110015**
info@christianworldimprints.com
www.ChristianWorldImprints.com
More at: www.kkagencies.co.in/sitemap
Phone: +91 11 25465925 Fax: +91 11 25173055

ISBN-13: 978-81-925121-3-6   ISBN-10: 81-925121-3-4

Cataloging in Publication Data--DK
Courtesy: D.K. Agencies (P) Ltd. <docinfo@dkagencies.com>

Miller, Robert D., II.
    The psalms as Israel's prayer and our own / Robert D.
Miller II.
        p.   cm. -- (Christian heritage rediscovered ; 2)
    Includes index.
    ISBN 9788192512136

    1. Bible. Psalms--Criticism, interpretation, etc. 2.
Prayer--Judaism.   I. Bible. Psalms. English. Selections.
II. Title.   III. Series: Christian heritage rediscovered ; 2.

DDC 223.206   23

Printed in India.

Introduction

The goal of this booklet is to explore the Book of Psalms as the religious poetry of Jews and Christians. I hope to help you acquire a knowledge and appreciation of the Psalms in their original Israelite contexts and in their usage within Hebrew religion. We will not stop there, but will continue to study the Psalms in their usage in early Christianity and subsequent Christian spirituality. The psalmists model for us the whole range of human emotions and levels of communication with God. They sing hymns of praise to God, cry out against God, cry out to God for help and deliverance, invoke the wrath of God upon their enemies, and celebrate the sovereignty of God over all creation. In this booklet, we will examine critical methods for reading the text of the Book of Psalms and study the shape and story of the Book of Psalms. We will also explore how we might interpret and appropriate the shape and story of the Book of Psalms as the quintessential prayers for today, expressing the full gamut of human emotions.

In addition to the chapters of this booklet, you might want to have a Bible handy. It will not be necessary to have the Scriptures at hand as we proceed, since many Psalms are included here. Still, you may want your favourite Bible on hand. I will quote from several versions as we go on. When an entire Psalm is provided for you here, it is my own translation.

Contents

Introduction v

**Chapter One: The Shape and Story of the
Book of Psalms** 1

   WHAT ARE THE PSALMS? 1

   TECHNIQUES OF HEBREW POETRY 3

   HOW MANY PSALMS ARE THERE? 18

   THE NUMBERING OF THE PSALMS 20

   THE PSALM TITLES 22

   THE FIVE BOOKS 28

   CONCLUSION 30

   FOR FURTHER STUDY 30

Chapter Two: Methods for Reading the Psalms 33

   THE LITERARY GENRES OF THE
      BOOK OF PSALMS 33

   THE FORMS OF THESE GENRES 54

   WHY WERE THE PSALMS WRITTEN? 66

   FORM CRITICISM AND PSYCHOLOGY 68

   THE THEOLOGY OF THE BOOK OF PSALMS 70

   CONCLUSION 76

   FOR FURTHER STUDY 76

**Chapter Three: The Psalms as the Quintessential
   Prayers for Today** 77
   THE PSALMS IN THE NEW TESTAMENT 77
   THE EARLY CHURCH AND THE PSALMS 80
   PRAYING AND SINGING THE PSALMS 86
   CONCLUSION 98
   FOR FURTHER STUDY 98

Index 99

Chapter One

The Shape and Story of the Book of Psalms

WHAT ARE THE PSALMS?

Apart from the Book of Psalms, most of the Old Testament comes to us as God's word to Israel. The Pentateuch, the first five books of the Bible that Israel called the "Torah", contains God's covenants He has made with Israel. The Historical books, such as Joshua and Judges, as well as the short narratives like Esther and Ruth, contain divinely inspired accounts of Israel's faith. In all of these, both Israel and God are spoken of in the third person: "He" did such, and "they" did so. In the prophetic books and in many of the wisdom books like Proverbs, the words are God's, and the revelation is direct. God is in the first person, "I", and Israel is in the second person, "you". Most of the Psalms, however, are different. The roles are reversed. God is the "you", and the author of the Psalm (or its reader) is the "I". Yet we know that the Psalms, as part of the canonical Scriptures, are a revelation inspired by God. They are words inspired by God that are addressed to God. You might want to begin this study of the Psalms by asking yourself in what sense, then, the Psalms are revelation. What does God want to reveal to us by "putting words in our mouth?" It is a question we will keep coming back to.

What are Psalms? The Hebrew name for the book is *tehillim*, which means "praises"; the word is related to "Hallelujah". Clearly, some of the Psalms are not quite praises – some are complaints. The name "Psalms" comes from the Greek name for the book, *Psalmoi*, which means, "sung to stringed instruments". While that may not always be accurate, it does capture the fact that Psalms are songs. As we shall see, many are even given musical commentary.

Think about this: why would one pray in poetry? What does poetry enable a prayer to capture that prose would not? And the Psalms are not just poetry; they are the lyrics to songs. This presents problems for our interpretation of them. Imagine taking a hymnal from your church and simply reading a hymn's words as if they were not lyrics but just sentences! There would be many problems in trying to understand what the intended meaning was. We are in a similar situation with the Psalms, since we will never know just how they were to be sung. We need to keep reminding ourselves that we are reading lyrics. As we will see in the third chapter, Christian tradition has always been that the best way to pray the Psalms is to sing them.

TECHNIQUES OF HEBREW POETRY

The Psalms are poetry set to music. But to us they do not look like poetry or lyrics. Much of our poetry and nearly all of our lyrics have rhyme. Typically, the ends of lines or clauses rhyme. The Psalms do not rhyme, even in the original Hebrew. (There are really two exceptions to that, Psalms 3:2 and 102:6 do seem to use rhyme.)

Meter

The Psalms, and all Hebrew poetry, do, however, have metric rhythm. We are acquainted with poetry that uses meter instead of rhyme in the form of the haiku or iambic pentameter. In Hebrew poetry, each line of poetry, which usually means each verse, has one or more "members". These are often called "stichs", and they are usually printed as separate lines of text in modern Bibles. So a verse can have one stich, two stichs (which is most common), or three or more.

Look at Psalm 113:

PSALM 113

[1]Hallelujah!
Praise, you servants of the LORD,
praise the name "Yahweh".

[2]Blessed be the name "Yahweh"
both now and forever.

[3]From the rising of the sun to its setting
let the name "Yahweh" be praised.

[4]High above all nations is the LORD;
above the heavens His glory.

[5]Who is like the LORD our God,
enthroned on high,

[6]Looking down on heaven and earth?

[7]The LORD raises the destitute from the dust,
lifts the poor from the garbage heap,

[8]Seats them with princes,
the princes of the people,

[9]Gives the childless wife a household,
As the joyful mother of children.
Hallelujah!

Verse 1 has three stichs: "Hallelujah", "Praise, you servants of the Lord", and "praise the name 'Yahweh.'" The rest of the verses of the Psalm have two stichs each, except the last verse, which again has three.

The meter or rhythm is based on number of accented syllables or stressed words in each stich. The most common meter is "3/3", or a stich with three emphasized syllables followed by another with three, the two stichs making up one verse. Often you can even see this in English translation. Look at Psalm 26:2. The stresses appear as "PROVE me, oh, LORD, and TRY me", three, and "TEST my HEART and MIND", three.

Another common meter is 3/2, three accents in the first line of the verse and two in the second. This rhythm is often found in laments. Look at Psalm 5, which is a lament. The opening verse shows the rhythm "GIVE EAR to my WORDS, oh, LORD; GIVE-HEED to my SIGHING". That is 3/2. Perhaps the "missing accent" in the second line conveys sense of something lost, much as a minor key conveys to us a sense of melancholy. This 3/2 meter is also found in 2 Sam 1:19-26, in David's lament over the deaths of Saul and Jonathan.

Other Psalms where you might be able to see the meter in English include Psalms 3 and 149. In many languages and cultures of the world today, certain poems or song genres are marked by a particular rhythm or accent sequence. It might be possible for those composing hymns today to use some of those genres or rhythmic patterns as models, especially if the hymns are derived from specific Psalms.

Parallelism

The most important feature of Hebrew poetry, however, is not the meter. What makes Hebrew poetry poetry is something called Parallelism. Parallelism is a correspondence of lines or stichs thru syntax, morphology, or meaning. It was first extensively studied by an Anglican Bishop named Robert Lowth who lived from 1710-1787.

The idea in parallelism is basically saying the same thing over again in different words. A quick glance through the Book of Psalms will show you that most Psalms do this with almost every pair of verses. In Psalm 3, "O Lord, how many are my foes" is rephrased in "Many are rising against me". Psalm 5 begins with "Give ear to my words, O Lord", restated as "Give heed to my sighing".

Types

Parallelism can be lumped into two types. Synonymous parallelism is when the second line echoes the same thought as the first. "A is so, what's more, B is so". In Psalm 113:7, the elements in the first stich are replaced with synonyms in the second stich: "raises" becomes "lifts", "destitute" becomes "poor", and "dust" becomes "garbage heap". Another way to do this is for a simile in the first stich to balance a reality in the human sphere in the second stich: "Like a doe goes to water; So a man to the Word".

The other type is Antithetic parallelism. The second stich presents a thought opposite to the first. An example is Psalm 75:10, where the "horns of the wicked are cut off" but "the horns of the righteous exalted". Psalm 126:5 shows another kind of antithetic parallelism, where the present is contrasted with the future.

Patterns and Applications

Parallelism can get a little fancy. Let us say there are two thoughts in two verses of a Psalm, "A" and "B". In parallelism, each thought will be restated, usually in the stich that immediately follows. A pattern like this could be called "AABB". But one could also put A's parallel stich after the B stichs, "ABBA". The Psalmists loved to do such things, sometimes extending the "pattern" out several stichs or verses, "ABCDDCBA" instead of "AABBCCDD".

They do this kind of thing not to be clever, but usually to emphasize a key meaning in the Psalm. In the example I just gave, idea "D" might be the main point of the Psalm or idea "A" might be, as a kind of introduction and conclusion. There is no end to the varieties of how the matches can be arranged.

We will now walk through identifying such patterns in a specific Psalm. Here is Psalm 22; rather than read it through, turn to page 9, and we will go through its parts one by one:

PSALM 22

For the leader; according to "The deer of the dawn". A Psalm of David.[*]

[1]My God, my God, why have you forsaken me?
Why are you so far from my cry for help,
from my wails of anguish?

[2]My God, I call by day, but you do not answer;
by night, but I have no relief.

[3]Yet you are enthroned as the Holy One;
you are the glory of Israel.

[4]In you our ancestors trusted;
they trusted and you rescued them.

[5]To you they cried out and they escaped;
in you, they trusted and were not disappointed.

[6]But I am a worm, hardly human,
scorned by everyone, despised by the people.

[7]All who see me mock me;
they sneer and they jeer;
they shake their heads at me.

---

[*] Do not worry about this "title" for now. We will explore these in later pages.

[8]"You relied on the LORD—let Him deliver you;
if He loves you, let Him rescue you".

[9]Yet you drew me forth from the womb,
made me safe at my mother's breast.

[10]Upon you I was laid from the womb;
since birth, you are my God.

[11]Do not remain so remote from me,
for trouble is near,
and there is no one to help.

[12]Many bulls surround me;
fierce Bashan Bulls encircle me.

[13]They open their mouths against me,
lions that rend and roar.

[14]Like water my life drains away;
all my bones wilt.
My heart has become wax,
it melts away within me.

[15]As dry as a potsherd is my throat;
my tongue sticks to my palate;
you lay me in the dust of death.

[16]Many dogs surround me;
a pack of evildoers closes in on me.
So wasted are my hands and feet.

[17]That I can count all my bones.
They stare at me and gloat;

[18]They divide my garments among them;
for my clothing, they cast lots.

[19]But you, LORD, do not stay far off;
my strength, come quickly to help me.

[20]Deliver me from the sword,
my forlorn life from the dog's teeth.

[21]Save me from the lion's mouth,
my poor life from the wild bulls' horns.

[22]Then I will proclaim your name to the assembly;
in the community, I will praise you.

[23]"You who revere the LORD, give praise!"
All descendants of Jacob, give glory;
show reverence, all descendants of Israel!

[24]For God has not ignored or scorned
the misery of this poor wretch,
Did not turn away from me,
but heard me when I cried out.

[25]I will offer praise in the great assembly;
my vows I will fulfil before those who revere Him.

[26]The poor will eat their fill;
those who seek the LORD will offer praise.
"May your hearts enjoy life forever!"

²⁷All the ends of the earth
will worship and turn to the LORD;
All the families of nations
will bow low before you.

²⁸For kingship belongs to the LORD,
the ruler over the nations.

²⁹All who sleep in the earth
will bow low before God;
All who have gone down into the dust
will kneel in homage.

³⁰And I will live for the LORD;
my descendants will serve you.

³¹A generation to come will be told of the Lord,
that they may proclaim to a people yet unborn
the deliverance you have brought.

Can you identify words in verses 1 and 11 that correspond to each other in some way, whether by similarity or contrast? What point is being emphasized by the speaker of these words? What is his purpose in saying them? That is, what is the function of the words? There are other examples of such patterns in Psalm 22. Compare verses 12-13 with verse 21. The next pair is verses 21 and 31. What do you notice about the way in which the pairs divide Psalm 22? Between which two verses does the major break of the Psalm occur? What is the prominent shift found at this juncture?

Now we will try it for Psalm 20.

PSALM 20

For the leader. A Psalm of David.

¹May the LORD answer you in time of turmoil;
the name of the God of Jacob defend you!

²May He send you help from the sanctuary,
from Zion be your support.

³May He remember your every offering,
graciously accept your sacrifice,
Selah

⁴May He grant what is in your heart,
fulfil your every dream.

⁵May we shout for joy at your victory,
raise banners in the name of our God.
The LORD grant your every prayer!

⁶Now I know the LORD gives victory
to His anointed.
He will answer him from the holy heavens
with a strong arm that brings victory.

⁷Some rely on chariots, others on horses,
but we, on the name of our God, "Yahweh".

⁸They collapse and crash,
but we stand strong and secure.

⁹LORD, grant victory to the king;
answer when we call upon you.

Look at the parallels of verses 4 and 5. Here the parallel serves to mark off a much smaller unit within the Psalm, one that corresponds to a paragraph in prose. In poetry, such a unit is called a stanza. If we consider Psalm 20 as a whole, we reasonably conclude that the corresponding words of verse 4 and verse 5 represent its central theme or main point. This suggestion is reinforced by another similar inclusion that bounds the Psalm as a whole, in verses 1 and 9. In this case, the inclusion reveals to whom the pronoun "you" refers. What does that tell us about the special function of this Psalm?

As you can see, being able to see the parallelism and to "read the patterns" can show you what the themes and main ideas of the Psalm are. Parallelism is also useful for finding the meaning of unclear words, since the words in one stich will "match" words in the next. There is a very good example of another way parallelism can help interpret a Psalm. Take Psalm 137:

PSALM 137

[1]By the rivers of Babylon
There we sat weeping
when we remembered Zion.

[2]On the poplars in its midst
we hung up our harps.

³For there our captors asked us
for the words of song;
Our tormentors, for joy:
"Sing for us a song of Zion!"

⁴But how could we sing the LORD's song
in a foreign land?

⁵If I forget you, Jerusalem,
may my right hand forget its skill.

⁶May my tongue stick to my palate
if I do not remember you,
If I do not exalt Jerusalem
as my greatest delight.

⁷Remember, LORD, against Edom
that day at Jerusalem.
They said: "Level it, level it
down to its foundations!"

⁸Fair Babylon the damned,
happy the one who pays you back
what you have done us!

⁹Happy the one who seizes your babies
and smashes them against the rock.

This beautiful Psalm ends with a rather startling plea for the killing of Babylonian children in verse 9. But a look at parallelism tells us there is more here than meets the eye. The difficult verse reads, "Happy shall they be who seizes your babies and

smashes them against the rock!" There appears
to be parallelism starting with verse 8, "Happy the
one who...", but then the ending is different. Yet we
know from parallelism that it should not be. The
remaining element in verse 8, "pays you back what
you have done to us" has to mean the same thing
as "seizes your babies and smashes them against
the rock". That means that the Psalm is not really
about Babylonian babies at all. It is about Israelite
babies. Their own children had been slaughtered,
in Nebuchadnezzar's destruction of Jerusalem.
The mourning expressed in the first six verses of
the Psalm can still not bring them to speak directly
about this immense tragedy, and the only way
they can articulate their grief is as we have it in
verses 8-9.

Other Poetic Features

Some other poetic features sometimes occur in
the Psalms. Words can be repeated as a kind of
refrain. Psalm 136 shows this happening every two
lines:

PSALM 136

[1]Praise the LORD, for He is good;
His love endures forever;

[2]Praise the God of gods;
His love endures forever;

³Praise the Lord of lords;
His love endures forever;

⁴Who alone has done great wonders,
His love endures forever;

⁵Who skilfully made the heavens,
His love endures forever;

⁶Who spread the earth upon the waters,
His love endures forever;

⁷Who made the great lights,
His love endures forever;

⁸The sun to rule the day,
His love endures forever;

⁹The moon and stars to rule the night,
His love endures forever;

¹⁰Who struck down the firstborn of Egypt,
His love endures forever;

¹¹And led Israel from their midst,
His love endures forever;

¹²With mighty hand and outstretched arm,
His love endures forever;

¹³Who split the Red Sea in two,
His love endures forever;

¹⁴And led Israel through,
His love endures forever;

[15]But swept Pharaoh and His army into the
Red Sea,
His love endures forever;

[16]Who led the people through the desert,
His love endures forever;

[17]Who struck down great kings,
His love endures forever;

[18]Slew powerful kings,
His love endures forever;

[19]Sihon, king of the Amorites,
His love endures forever;

[20]Og, king of Bashan,
His love endures forever;

[21]And made their lands an inheritance,
His love endures forever;

[22]An inheritance for Israel, His servant,
His love endures forever;

[23]The LORD remembered us in our indigence,
His love endures forever;

[24]Freed us from our foes,
His love endures forever;

[25]And gives food to all flesh,
His love endures forever;

[26]Praise the God of heaven,
His love endures forever.

Psalms 42 and 43 share the same "chorus" in 42:5, 11 and 43:5, indicating that it is probably just one long Psalm.

The Psalms are also full of figurative language. There are metaphors that refer to Hebrew customs, like "anoint my head with oil" (Psalm 23:5), or that make sense in many cultures, like "bridle my mouth" (39:1). Psalm 85:10-11 is a particularly difficult passage to translate, as concepts like hope are personified.

Another technique the Hebrew poets used occasionally was the acrostic. An acrostic is where each successive line of a Psalm begins with successive letters of the alphabet. The first stich of verse one begins with *aleph* (Hebrew "A"), the second stich with *bet* ("B"), and so on. This is obviously difficult to duplicate in the English translations, but the New Jerusalem Bible tries for Psalm 25. Other acrostics are Psalms 34, 111, 112 and 145. In Psalm 119, each *paragraph* begins with a successive letter of the alphabet. In fact, every line from a given paragraph starts with that letter; the first paragraph all lines start with *aleph*, in the second with *bet*, and so on.

HOW MANY PSALMS ARE THERE?

Several ancient texts of the Old Testament actually contain 151 Psalms. The Septuagint, which was a

Greek translation of the Bible made by Jews in Egypt a century or two before the time of Christ, had a "Psalm 151". It is also found in the Old Latin Bibles that were around before St. Jerome produced the Vulgate, and in the Syriac-language Bibles that were used in the Middle East. The Eastern Orthodox Church actually considers Psalm 151 canonical. The Syriac Bibles also had four more Psalms, Psalms 152-155.

The discovery of the Dead Sea Scrolls, beginning in 1948, revolutionized biblical studies. By giving us texts of the Old Testament that were far older than anything else still in existence, they enabled scholars to get much closer to the original forms of the text. There were two scrolls of Psalms found in the Dead Sea Scrolls. Both had been written between 1 AD and 50 AD.

What they showed was startling. One of the scrolls contained forty of the Psalms found between Psalm 90 and Psalm 150, but in a different order. It also contained Psalm 151 and two of the Psalms that were known from the Syriac Bible. This showed first that these "extra" Psalms were not added to the Book of Psalms later. In fact, they were even older than the arrangement of the Psalms was. They also showed that the arrangement of the Psalms was a very late development. If you think about it, the ordering of the Psalms could be arbitrary. If I ask you "What hymn comes after *Where Charity and*

Love Prevail?" you will not be able to answer me because the order differs in different hymnals. The Book of Psalms must have been like that, too; for many centuries, the order did not really matter.

The second Psalms scroll contained all of Psalms 1-69 in the same order we now have them, followed by Psalms 91-92, 94, 99-100, 102-103, 112, 116, and 118. There were no holes or tears between those Psalms, they simply were not present. This adds more to our understanding. It means that the order was beginning to take shape at the time of Christ. The first sixty-nine Psalms are exactly as today and the ones from there on are in the right order, even if they are not all there. Both scrolls show us that it was not set by the time of Christ just what Psalms belonged in the canonical collection.

THE NUMBERING OF THE PSALMS

The Septuagint has all of the Psalms in the same order we are used to, except for having additional Psalms at the end. But the numbering of the Psalms is different. In the Septuagint, what we call Psalm 10 is given as the last verses of a doubly long Psalm 9. This makes good sense, as Psalm 10 completes the acrostic begun in Psalm 9. However, it causes the numbering of the Psalms to be off by one; thus, what we call Psalm 23 is called Psalm 22 in the Septuagint. Then what we call Psalm 115 is given as the "last verses" of the Septuagint's long Psalm 113 (our 114). This would leave us at two behind, but fortunately, the Septuagint splits our Psalm 116 in two, numbering it as 114 and 115. That returns us to one behind. The Septuagint also splits 147 into two (146 and 147), thus returning the numbering to same as ours.

While this may seem convoluted and trivial, it is important, because St. Jerome used the Septuagint numbering in His Vulgate. From that point on, Medieval commentators kept the Septuagint-Vulgate numbering. So if St. Bernard says something about the "22nd Psalm", he means the one that begins "The Lord is my shepherd" – our 23rd Psalm. It can be very confusing if the Psalm is just referred to by number and not quoted. You may have an older Bible that uses the alternate numbering, which was only abandoned in the 20th century in the Catholic Church. Often to avoid confusion a writer will give both numbers: "In Psalm 23 (22), we read..." With some modern Bibles, there is also some confusion about the verse numbering. In Hebrew, the "titles" of the Psalms are numbered as verse 1. The Septuagint placed the titles separately above each Psalm, and never numbered them as verses. Almost all modern English Bibles follow the Septuagint on this, and give the titles without verse numbers, starting with verse 1 for the Psalm itself. There is good reason for this choice, because as we will see the titles are not integral parts of the Psalms. The only Bible that numbers the titles the way the Hebrew does is the New American Bible (NAB), the official translation of the Catholic Church in the United States. If you are using the NAB, we will be left with my verse 1 often being your verse 2. Not every Psalm has a title, so you cannot make a blanket policy of assuming the numbers are off by one. I will be using my own translation for most of this booklet, which follows the typical English numbering, so if you are using the New American be aware that we may not be in the same verse.

THE PSALM TITLES

These "titles" we just referred to deserve more attention. One hundred sixteen of the Psalms have titles, including almost all of the Psalms 1-89. Do you remember that break? One of the Psalms scrolls from the Dead Sea Scrolls only contained the Psalms following 1-89. Of the thirty-four Psalms that do not have titles, twenty-one of them do have titles in the Septuagint. Often the Septuagint title is simply the last verse of the preceding Psalm moved over, but the Septuagint also alters some of the titles from the Hebrew, usually by lengthening them.

Attributional Authorship

PSALMS OF DAVID

Now we can look at the nature of these titles. Many of the titles seem to be attributing authorship to specific people, most commonly to King David. Many of these also give a situation in David's life when the Psalm was written.

Seventy-three Psalms are attributed to David. There are, however, many problems with suggesting David wrote these Psalms. The text of "David's" Psalms often speak of things that did not exist until long after David: the Temple in 3:4; 5:7; 18:6; 28:2; 24:7-9; 122:1; a prayer to rebuild Jerusalem in 51:18. There are also cases where the story presented in the title clashes with the way the story is told in the Old Testament Historical books. What is said about "Abimelech" in Psalm 34 is really about a man named "Achish" in 1 Sam 21:14. The title Psalm 60 -- "When David fought the Arameans of Northwest Mesopotamia and Zobah, and when Joab returned and defeated twelve thousand Edomites at the Valley of Salt"-- describes events totally differently from 2 Sam 8:13 and 1 Chron 18:12. The figure should be 18,000 not 12,000, and in Samuel it is David who kills the Edomites, in Chronicles Abishai, but never Joab. Sometimes single Psalm is given more than one author, as in

Psalm 88. Perhaps something else is going on with the titles.

We have already seen how the titles were very flexible between the Septuagint and the Hebrew Old Testament, even when every other verse of the Psalm was identical. Even in the Hebrew, the title is missing in some manuscripts for Psalms 108, 122, 124, 127, 131, 133, and 138. We might even say the titles' presence is tendentious, which is why they are not given verse numbers (and, in fact, two modern versions, the Revised English Bible and the Today's English Version, omit them entirely).

Now when a title says "A Psalm of David", the "of" is just as ambiguous in Hebrew as it is in English. The preposition translated "of" can mean "by", "by David". But the preposition can also be translated as "to" or "for", as in "dedicated to David", or as "about", "A Psalm About David". We could possibly conclude that a Psalm could be about or dedicated to David in honour of the specific event from His life that is mentioned.

COLLECTIONS IN THE BOOK OF PSALMS

But it is also possible that there is more to it. Besides David, there are also Psalms attributed to the "Sons of Korah" (Korah was Aaron's cousin who was swallowed up by the earth in the desert for challenging Moses), and Asaph (a Levite singer in the time of David), Solomon, and one each to Moses, Heman, and Ethan. The Sons of Korah, Ethan, and Heman were, according to the book of Chronicles, priest-cantors at the time of David and Solomon. So with the exception of Moses, all the Psalm titles refer to David and His contemporaries.

The "David" Psalms are not scattered about, but cluster in four collections. The first is Psalms 3-41, excluding only 10 (which, as we saw, is really part of 9) and 33. The second collection is 51-71. Lacking David titles are 66-67 and 71-72, but we do not say the collection ends at 70 because 72:20 says, "The Prayers of David, son of Jesse, are ended". Of course, they are not ended; there are two more collections in 108-110 and 138-145.

The Sons of Korah Psalms are in two collections, 42-49 – although not 43, which is really a continuation of 42 -- and 84-88.The Asaph Psalms are 50 and 73-83.

So the Psalms titles that identify individuals are actually an organizing structure for the Book of Psalms. Since two of these collections (and two stray Psalms for Heman and Ethan) bear the names of the ancestors of the guilds of temple singers, many scholars have concluded that the collections are Psalms "for" them, belong to them, and form part of their repertoire. It makes sense that the particular official repertoire of individual families would be attached to one of the ancestors of that family. It is possible, then, that we are looking at the building blocks of the Book of Psalms, earlier shorter collections of Psalms, particular to different groups of Temple singers, that were later joined together in one volume.

Musical Notation

TYPES OF COMPOSITIONS

There are other kinds of titles. Many relate to the performance of the Psalm. Some indicate the type of composition the Psalm is, although we cannot really decipher most of them. Some English Bibles offer translations for these terms, others just write the Hebrew term in Western letters. What most Bibles translate as "a Psalm", for example, is *mizmor*. We saw that "Psalm" is not really an English word but comes from the Greek "stringed instruments". It is not really a good translation for *mizmor*, which likely means something about modulation. Other Psalms are called *maskil*. There is a group of these around Psalm 55. Most Bibles leave this untranslated; the New King James renders it "a Contemplation", following the Septuagint, and the New Jerusalem has "a Poem". There is also the *miktam* (e.g., Psalms 16, 57, 60). The New Jerusalem has it "In a Quiet Voice", which is definitely wrong since 57:2 speaks of "crying out". The *Shiggaion* (Psalm 7) is probably as the New American has it, "a lament".

TUNES

Some titles give the tune to which the Psalm goes (e.g., Psalms 57-59). Psalms are to be sung "to the tune of" "Lilies" (Psalm 80), "The Deer of Dawn" (Psalm 22), and others. We have no idea what these ancient tunes were and no record of them outside of the Psalms.

LITURGICAL USE

A few titles tell the liturgical use for the Psalm - "For the Sabbath" or "For the Memorial Offering". Psalms 120-134 are called "Psalms of Degrees". Christian tradition called them the "Gradual Psalms". This title could also be translated as "Psalms of Ascents", meaning Psalms for the ascending pilgrimages to Jerusalem. That seems to be the theme in Psalms 122 and 126, although it does not work for Psalms 130-131.

INSTRUMENTATION

Fifty-five Psalms are entitled, "for the leader" or "choirmaster". Psalm 46 is likely to be translated "for the sopranos". Seven Psalms are "with stringed instruments" and Psalm 5 is "for the Flutes". Musical indications also occur within Psalms. There are seventy-one places in thirty-nine Psalms were the word *Selah* appears. It is likely a place for an instrumental interlude, as the Septuagint understood it, or a complete "rest" from singing and playing, as St. Gregory of Nyssa interpreted it.

Archaeological discoveries and texts from other ancient Middle Eastern cultures have taught us a great deal about ancient Israelite music. Although many of the terms in the Psalms remain untranslatable, we can make some good estimations of what kind of instruments would have been used. The flutes of Psalm 5 for instance, were probably tuned to diatonic scales; some produced successive chromatic tones, some the entire 12 degrees of the octave.

There were two kinds of stringed instruments. Both are hand-held and consecutively strung with gut. The older of the two is the *kinnor* or lyre. It had eight or ten strings and a velvety timbre. You played it by scraping all the strings while muting some with left hand. Incidentally, one of the ancient names for the Sea of Galilee was the Sea of Kinnereth, because it is shaped like a lyre. The other stringed instrument was the harp, either ten- or twelve-stringed.

THE FIVE BOOKS

To return once more to our study of the assembly of the Book of Psalms, there is another kind of grouping or division in the Book of Psalms other than the title collections. These are what are known as the "five books". They were noted in the early 3rd century AD by St. Hippolytus of Rome, in 300 AD by St. Jerome citing an earlier Jewish tradition, and by other early Christians. What they noticed was a doxology that was repeated in very similar words in Psalm 41:13; 72:18-19; 89:52 and 106:48. Interpreting those doxologies as the ends of groupings of Psalms, five "books" result. Psalm 150 in its entirety serves as the final doxology. So certain are most scholars of the existence of these "five books" that since 1881 most English editions have indicated them.

The first book thus is Psalms 1-41. After Psalms 1 and 2, this is precisely the first "David title" collection. This cannot be a coincidence and is probably evidence of an early "seam" between once-separate parts of the Book of Psalms. The second Book is Psalms 42-72. The third is Psalms 73-89. The break after Psalm 89 we have seen twice already, as marking the start of the first Psalms Dead Sea Scroll and the end of the concentration of titles. Book four is Psalms 90-106, and book five is 107-150.

Some of these divisions were certainly old joints between volumes, as with the 41/42 break and the 89/90 break. Others may have been superimposed later over already-joined title collections. Psalms 106 and 107 begin identically, and this might indicate that they are not from two different sources. The present arrangement of five books is most assuredly meant to parallel the five books of the Pentateuch.

CONCLUSION

We have seen the nature of Hebrew poetry and how features like parallelism are important for interpreting a Psalm. We have tried to explain the titles that are attached to the Psalms, and all along the way, we have gained insights into how the Book of Psalms came to be. We will further pursue that issue in the next chapter.

FOR FURTHER STUDY

By way of a practical application of this chapter, let us try some of the following when next prayerfully reading the Psalms:

Become accustomed to "reading" the parallelism. Look for ideas repeated at the start and finish of the Psalm that will tell you the main idea, and find a verse in the middle without parallelism that might be a key idea to meditate on longer.

Consider praying a group of Psalms that are all given similar titles. For example, you might choose to mediate on the Sons of Korah Psalms over a period of days. You may be surprised at the moods and themes this highlights. The same could be done by reading a single "book", going in order.

In a hymnal, locate a hymn that is derived from a Psalm. Then – as you are able and quietly – sing the Psalm-hymn as prayer.

Chapter Two

Methods for Reading the Psalms

THE LITERARY GENRES OF THE BOOK OF PSALMS

The main way in which scholars study the Psalms is what is known as "Form Criticism". It begins with dividing the Psalms according to their different genres, and this is done by exploring three questions.

The first question is to ask who is addressed in the Psalm. As we said in the first chapter, most often it is God that is being addressed. There are some Psalms, such as Psalm 1, where this is not the case. So we can divide the Psalms first in two: those addressed to God and all the rest. For now, let us continue with the ones addressed to God, which are the majority.

The Major Genres

The second question is to ask who is speaking. St. Hilary of Poitiers (d. 367) said, "The primary condition of knowledge for reading the Psalms is the ability to see as whose mouthpiece we are to regard the Psalmist as speaking, and who is it that he addresses" (*Homilies on the Psalms* 1). Since the 1930s, biblical scholars have answered this question in three ways: either it is an individual speaking, or it is a group, or it is the king, who somewhat speaks for the nation and as an individual. All the Psalms addressed to God, then, can be categorized as Individual Psalms, Collective (or Communal) Psalms, and Royal Psalms.

The third question is "What is the intent of the speaker?" Again, the small range of answers was put forward in the 1930s and is still used. The Psalms are laments, thanksgivings, or hymns. How is a hymn different from a thanksgiving? A hymn praises God in general terms for His greatness and faithfulness as creator and ruler of the Universe, while a thanksgiving thanks God for specific past deliverance or compassion. As with the second question, this is not really new; St. Athanasius of Alexandria (d. 373) also separated the Psalms into thanksgivings, laments, and so forth (*Letter to Marcellinus*, 111-113).

Putting this all together, the Psalms addressed to God can be Individual, Collective, or Royal Hymns, Thanksgivings, or Laments, although not all of these nine types are found. An example of a Collective Hymn would be Psalm 100:

PSALM 100

A Psalm for giving thanks. [Remember these titles are ancient and do not correspond to the categories we are using; this is not a Thanksgiving.]

[1]Shout joyfully to the LORD, all you lands;

[2]Worship the LORD with glad shouts;
approach Him with jubilant song.

[3]Know that the LORD is God,
our maker to whom we belong,
whose people we are, God's well-tended flock.

[4]Enter His gates with thanksgiving,
His courts with praise.
Give thanks to Him, bless His name;

[5]Good indeed is the LORD,
Whose love endures forever,
whose faithfulness lasts through every generation.

"*Our maker*". It is actually very easy to identify the types. Telling collective from individual is simply a matter of I/me/my or us/we/our. Laments are easy to tell from hymns and thanksgivings, which are admittedly harder to tell apart at times. Individual Thanksgivings include Psalms 30, 32, 34, 92, and 116. Here is Psalm 30:

PSALM 30

A Psalm. A song for the dedication of the Temple. Of David.

[1]I praise you, LORD, for you picked me up and did not let my enemies gloat over me.

[2]O LORD, my God,
I cried to you for help and you healed me.

[3]LORD, you brought my soul up from the tomb;
from going down to the pit,
you let me live.

[4]Sing praise to the LORD, you faithful;
give thanks to His holy memory.

[5]For His anger lasts but a moment;
His favour a lifetime.
At dusk, weeping comes for the night;
but at dawn, there is rejoicing.

[6]Complacent, I once said,
"I shall never be shaken".

⁷LORD, you showed me favour,
Established mountains of virtue for me,
But when you hid your face
I was hit with fear.

⁸To you, LORD, I cried out;
with the Lord, I pleaded for mercy.

⁹"What gain is there from my lifeblood,
from me going down to the grave?
Does dust give you thanks
or declare your probity?

¹⁰Hear, O LORD, have mercy on me;
LORD, be my helper".

¹¹You turned my tears into dancing;
you removed my sackcloth
and clothed me with gladness.

¹²So that my glory may praise you
and not be silent;
O LORD, my God,
forever will I give you thanks.

Collective Thanksgivings include 107, 124, and 135. Psalm 2 is usually considered a Royal Thanksgiving, since verse 7 fits best in the mouth of the king. Psalms 18 and 21 are also considered Royal.

PSALM 18

For the leader. Of David, the servant of the
LORD, who sang to the LORD the words of this
song after the LORD had rescued him from the
clutches of all His enemies and from the hand
of Saul.

[1]He said:
I love you, LORD, my strength,

[2]LORD, my rock, my fortress, my champion,
my God, my rock of refuge,
my shield, my saving horn, my stronghold!

[3]Praised be the LORD, I shout!
I have been saved from my enemies.

[4]The cords of death ensnared me;
the floods of chaos terrified me.

[5] The cords of the grave encircled me;
the snares of death lay in wait for me.

[6] In my fear, I called out: "LORD!"
I cried out to my God.
From His temple, He heard my voice;
my cry to Him reached His ears.

[7]The earth rocked and shook;
the foundations of the mountains shuddered;
they quaked as His wrath flared up.

⁸Smoke rose from His nostrils,
a devouring fire from His mouth;
it kindled coals into flame.

⁹He parted the heavens and descended,
a thundercloud under His feet.

¹⁰Mounted on cherubim He flew,
borne along on the wings of the wind.

¹¹He made darkness His cloak around Him;
water-darkened storm clouds His mantle.

¹²From the flash before Him, His clouds passed,
hail and fiery coals.

¹³The LORD thundered from heaven;
the Most High's voice boomed.

¹⁴ He let fly His arrows and scattered them;
Shot His lightning bolts and dispersed them.

¹⁵Then the seabed was exposed;
the world's foundations lay bare,
At your rebuke, O LORD,
at the storming breath of your nostrils.

¹⁶He reached down from on high and seized me;
drew me out of the deep waters.

¹⁷He rescued me from my mighty enemy,
from foes too powerful for me.

¹⁸They attacked me on my day of distress,
but the LORD was my support.

[19]He set me free in liberty;
He rescued me because He loves me.

[20]The LORD affirmed my righteousness,
rewarded my clean hands.

[21]For I kept the ways of the LORD;
I was loyal to my God.

[22]For His laws were all before me,
His decrees I did not discard.

[23]I was honest with Him;
vigilant against sin.

[24]So the LORD rewarded my righteousness,
the cleanness of my hands in His sight.

[25]Toward the faithful you are faithful;
to the honest, you are honest;

[26]Toward the pure, you are pure;
but to the devious, you are devious.

[27]For humble people you save;
haughty eyes you bring low.

[28]For you, LORD, give light to my lamp;
my God brightens my darkness.

[29]With you I can charge an armed band,
with help of my God, I can leap a wall.

[30]God's way is sure;
the LORD's promise is perfect;
he is a shield for all who take refuge in Him.

[31]Truly, who is God except the LORD?
Who but our God is the rock?

[32]This God who girded me with gusto,
kept my way sure,

[33]Who made my feet like a deer's,
And set me on the heights,

[34]Who trained my hands for war,
my arms to string a bronze bow.

[35]You gave me your saving shield;
your right hand upheld me;
your favour established my fame.

[36]You made way for my steps beneath me;
my ankles never twisted.

[37]I pursued my enemies and overtook them;
I did not turn back until I defeated them.

[38]I destroyed them; they could not rise;
they fell at my feet.

[39]You girded me with valour for war,
subjected my foes beneath me.

[40]You made my enemies expose their necks to
me;
those who hated me I silenced.

[41]They cried for help, but no one saved them;
cried to the LORD but got no answer.

⁴²I ground them to dust before the wind;
I left them like mud in the streets.

⁴³You rescued me from popular unrest;
made me head over nations.

⁴⁴A people I had not known served me;
as soon as they heard of me they obeyed.

⁴⁵Foreigners submitted before me;
foreigners cringed;
they came cowering from their dungeons.

⁴⁶The LORD lives! Blessed be my rock!
Exalted be God, my saviour!

⁴⁷O God who granted me vengeance,
made peoples subject to me,
and saved me from my enemies,

⁴⁸Truly, you have raised me above my foes,
from anarchists you have rescued me.

⁴⁹Thus I will praise you, LORD, among the
nations;
I will sing praises to your name.

⁵⁰You have given great victories to your king,
and shown mercy to your anointed,
to David and His descendants forever.

PSALM 21

For the leader. A Psalm of David.

[1]LORD, the king finds joy in your power;
in your victory how great His gladness!

[2]You have granted him His heart's desire;
you did not refuse the request of His lips.
Selah

[3]For you welcomed him with bountiful blessings;
you placed on His head a pure gold crown.

[4]He asked you for life;
And you gave it to him,
Days unending.

[5]Great is his glory in your victory;
majesty and grandeur you grant him.

[6]You make him the model of blessings forever,
you hearten him with the joy of your company.

[7]For the king trusts in the LORD,
stands firm through the Most High's mercy.

[8]Your hand will reach all your enemies;
your right hand will reach your foes!

[9]At the time of your coming
you will make them a bonfire.
Then the LORD in His anger will consume them,
devour them with fire.

¹⁰Even their descendants you will wipe out
from the earth,
their lineage from the human race.

¹¹Though they intend evil against you,
Concocting conspiracy, they will not succeed,

¹²For you will put them to flight;
you will aim at their faces with your bow.

¹³Arise, LORD, in your power!
We will heartily sing the praise of your might.

There are more Individual Laments than any other type. These are especially concentrated in Psalms 1-89, a division you will recall from Chapter One. These laments are typically bewailing sickness or false accusation. Examples include 22, 69, and 142. Collective Laments grieve over drought, famine, plague, and war, and examples are Psalms 44, 74, and 80. Psalm 89 is considered a Royal Lament, because of verses 19-41, as is Psalm 144.

It is possible that the thanksgivings and hymns are not really distinct, but a bigger question is with the royal Psalms. Psalms 2, 89, and 101 are called royal because the king is speaking, while Psalms 20 and 45 are called royal because they are addressed to the king. It seems that it might be easier to just stick with "individual" or "collective". As you can gather, assigning a genre label to a Psalm is not an objective and definitive task. Scholars disagree on what should be called what. There are several indexes of the Psalms with their genres labelled available online. If you are interested, you could go to http://freechristimages.org/biblebooks/Book_of_Psalms.htm among others.

If complaint and thanksgiving are most frequent, what is the basic theology of the Book of Psalms? It is very personal, very emotional. It is also very direct with God. He is thanked and complained to. He is near to His people and cares about their well-being, both communally and each individual. Remember that the Book of Psalms contains inspired prayers to God. This is how God wants us to approach Him, knowing He is a caring Father who is concerned about us.

Minor Genres

There are also minor forms, usually not addressed to God. Also included here are a few addressed to God that do not fit into the categories of lament, thanksgiving, and hymn.

As we saw in Chapter One, there are Pilgrimage Songs, such as Psalms 84 and 122: "Let us go to the house of the Lord!"

PSALM 84

For the leader; "upon the *gittith*". A Psalm of
the Sons of Korah.

¹How lovely your lodging,
O LORD of hosts!

²My soul yearns and longs
for the courts of the LORD.
My heart and flesh cry out
for the living God.

³As the sparrow finds a home
and the swallow a nest to settle her young,
My home is by your altars,
LORD of hosts, my king and my God!

⁴Happy are those who dwell in your house!
They never cease praising you.
Selah

⁵Happy are those who find refuge in you,
In whose hearts are pilgrimage roads.

⁶As they pass through the Valley of Tears,
they find spring water to drink.
The early rain covers it with blessings.

⁷They pass through outer and inner walls
and see the God of gods on Zion.

⁸LORD God of hosts, hear my prayer;
listen, God of Jacob.
Selah

⁹O God, watch over our royalty's coat of arms;
look upon the face of your anointed.

¹⁰Better one day in your courts
than a thousand elsewhere.
Better a doorstep of the house of my God
than a home in the tents of the wicked.

¹¹For the LORD God is a sun and shield,
bestowing all grace and glory.
The LORD withholds nothing good
from those who walk without blame.

¹²O LORD of hosts,
happy are those who trust in you!

PSALM 122

A song of ascents. Of David.

¹I rejoiced when they said to me,
"Let us go to the house of the LORD".

²And now our feet are standing
within your gates, O Jerusalem.

³Jerusalem, built as a city
walled round about.

⁴There the tribes have come,
the tribes of the LORD,
As it was commanded for Israel
to give thanks to the name of the LORD.

⁵There are the thrones of justice,
the thrones of the house of David.

⁶Pray for the peace of Jerusalem,
"May those who love you prosper!

⁷May peace be within your parapet,
prosperity within your towers".

⁸For the sake of my brothers, family, and
friends I say,
"Peace be with you".

⁹For the sake of the house of the LORD, our God,
I pray for your good.

These are not the only Psalms that are directly liturgical. Psalms 15 and 24 may have been liturgical music for entry into the Temple: "Who shall stand in His holy place?" Psalm 95 seems to have liturgical instructions included, too, "Come, let us worship and bow down".

PSALM 15

A Psalm of David.

¹LORD, who may linger in your tent?
Who may dwell on your holy mountain?

²Whoever walks without blame,
doing what is right,
speaking truth from the heart;

[3]Who does not malign with His tongue,
does no harm to a friend,
nor slanders a neighbour;

[4]Who spurns the wicked,
but reveres those who revere the LORD;
Who keeps a promise despite the cost,

[5]Lends no money at interest,
accepts no bribe against the innocent.
Whoever acts like this
Will never be shaken.

PSALM 24

A Psalm of David.

[1]The earth is the LORD's and all it holds,
the world and those who dwell in it.

[2]For He founded it on the seas,
established it over the rivers.

[3]Who may go up the mountain of the LORD?
Who can stand in His holy place?

[4]The clean of hand and pure of heart,
who has not handed His soul over to a lie,
who has not sworn falsely.

[5]He will receive blessings from the LORD,
and justice from His saving God.

⁶"Such is the generation that seeks Him,
that seeks the face of the God of Jacob".
Selah

⁷Lift up your heads, O gates;
be lifted, you ancient portals,
that the king of glory may enter.

⁸Who is this king of glory?
The LORD, a mighty warrior,
the LORD, mighty in battle.

⁹Lift up your heads, O gates;
rise up, you ancient portals,
that the king of glory may enter.

¹⁰Who is this king of glory?
The LORD of hosts, He is the king of glory.
Selah

There are Psalms that are addressed to oneself that we might call "Psalms of Confidence". These can be either collective, as in Psalm 46, or individual, as in 23, 62, 91, 121, and 131: "The Lord is my shepherd".

PSALM 46

¹For the leader. A song of the Korahites. For the sopranos.

²God is our refuge and our strength,
an ever-present help in distress.

³So we do not fear, though earth be shaken
and mountains quake from the dragon.

⁴Though his waters rage and foam
and mountains totter at his uproar.
Selah

⁵Streams of the river gladden the city of God,
the holy dwelling of the Most High.

⁶God is in its midst; it shall not be shaken;
God will help it at daybreak.

⁷Though nations rage and kingdoms totter,
He utters His voice and the earth melts.

⁸The LORD of hosts is with us;
our stronghold is the God of Jacob.
Selah

⁹Come and see the works of the LORD,
who has done fearsome deeds on earth;

¹⁰Who stops war as far as the ends of the earth,
breaks the bow, splinters the spear,
and burns the shields with fire;

¹¹"Be still and know that I am God!
I am exalted among the nations,
exalted on the earth".

¹²The LORD of hosts is with us;
our stronghold is the God of Jacob.
Selah

Some Psalms are called Wisdom Psalms because of the presence of ideas, linguistic, or stylistic features distinctive of wisdom literature like Proverbs or Job. The list of these varies widely among scholars, but most would include Psalms 1, 37, 49, and 112. Psalms 1 and 112 present "two ways", much like Proverbs. Psalms 37 and 49 ask, "Why do the wicked prosper?" much like Job and Ecclesiastes.

PSALM 112

[1]Hallelujah!
Happy the one who reveres the LORD,
who greatly delights in His decrees.

[2]His descendants shall be mighty on the land,
A righteous generation will be blessed.

[3]Wealth and riches shall be in his house;
His prosperity shall endure forever.

[4]Light shines through the darkness for the upright;
gracious, merciful, and righteous.

[5]It goes well for the man who lends generously,
who conducts his business justly.

[6]For he shall never be shaken;
the righteous shall be remembered forever.

[7]He shall not fear bad news;
his heart is steadfast, trusting the LORD.

[8]His heart is calm, without fear,
until at last he looks down on his foes.

[9] Lavishly he gives to the poor;
his prosperity shall endure forever;
his name shall be exalted in honour.

[10]The wicked sees and is angry;
Grinds his teeth and wastes away;
the cravings of the wicked come to nothing.

A minor genre that is addressed to God is the Confessional. These beautiful Psalms are known in Catholic tradition as the "Seven Penitential Psalms". They are Psalms 6, 32, 38, 51, 102, 130, and 143.

PSALM 130

A song of ascents.

[1]Out of the depths I call to you, LORD;

[2]Lord, hear my cry!
May your ears be alert
to my cry for mercy.

[3]LORD if you keep a record of our sins,
Lord, who could stand?

[4]But with you is forgiveness
and so you are revered.

[5]I wait for the LORD,
my soul waits
and I hope for His word.

⁶My soul looks for the Lord
more than sentinels for daybreak.
More than sentinels for daybreak,

⁷Let Israel hope in the LORD.
For with the LORD is mercy,
With Him is full liberation,

⁸And God will redeem Israel
from all its sins.

There are also recitals of Israel's History (Psalms 78, 105-6, 135-36) and even curses (Psalms 35 and 109), to which we will return in Chapter Three.

THE FORMS OF THESE GENRES

Now each of these distinct genres happens to have a distinct form. That is, there is a distinct structure or format for each genre. For example, the hymns all begin with a call to praise, then a motive introduced with "because" or "for", then a repeat of the call to praise. A clear example is Psalm 117, where verse 1 has the call to praise, then verse 2 begins with "for" and has the motive, ending with a renewed call to "Praise the Lord!"

Thanksgivings

Most of the forms are more complex, and it is very important to examine them. The thanksgivings have four parts. First, there is a declaration of thanks for specific divine acts or attributes. Second, there is a description of past distress. Third is a testimony of how God addressed that distress. And fourth, there is either a statement of praise or a promise to praise God in the future.

Psalm 116 is an example. The initial thanks is in verses 1 and 2. Then the past distress is described in verses 3 and 4. The testimony is not all in one place, but is found in verses 6 and 10-11. The promise to thank God is in verses 12-19.

PSALM 116

[1]I love the LORD, who listened
to my voice in supplication,

[2]Who turned an ear to me
on the day I called.

[3]I was caught by the traps of death;
the snares of Sheol had seized me;
I felt agony and dismay.

[4]Then I called on the name "Yahweh",
"O LORD, save my life!"

[5]The LORD gives freely and is righteous;
yes, our God is merciful.

[6]The LORD protects the simple;
I was helpless, but He saved me.

[7]Return to your rest, my soul;
the LORD has been very good to you.

⁸For my soul has been freed from death,
my eyes from tears, my feet from stumbling.

⁹ I shall walk before the LORD
in the land of the living.

¹⁰I kept faith, even when I said,
"I am greatly afflicted!"

¹¹I said in my alarm,
"All men are liars!"

¹²How can I repay the LORD
for all the great good done for me?

¹³ I will raise the Cup of Salvation
and call on the name "Yahweh".

¹⁴I will fulfil my promises to the LORD
in the presence of all His people.

¹⁵ Dear in the eyes of the LORD
is the death of His devoted one.

¹⁶LORD, I am your servant,
your servant, the child of your maidservant;
you have loosed my shackles.

¹⁷I will offer a sacrifice of thanksgiving
and call on the name "Yahweh".

¹⁸I will fulfil my promises to the LORD
in the presence of all His people,

¹⁹In the courts of the house of the LORD,
in your midst, O Jerusalem.
Hallelujah!

The pattern can take many verses to play out and can jump around. Psalm 18 (printed on page 38) begins with thanks in many of the same words as 116. This thanks is in verses 1-3. The past distress is in verses 4-5. The testimony, however, takes up all of verses 7 through 48. The promise to praise is in verse 49.

Laments

The lament has the most complex format. In its full form, it has seven parts. The formats are not wooden, and so some elements may be missing or not in the same order, but most often they are as listed here. First is a general call to God, usually using an imperative of "hear", "listen", or "heed". Following this appeal, the problem is spelled out. The third element is a request, a petition usually formulated in the imperative ("save!"). Fourth is an avowal of innocence by the lamenter, or sometimes a confession of guilt. Fifth, the speaker professes their trust in God to save them. Sixth is a promise to thank God when saved. And seventh is actual praise of God.

Psalm 69 shows these elements clearly, although the order varies. The appeal is in verse 1, "Save me, O God". The problem is spelled out in verses 2-4. There is both an avowal of innocence in the last line of verse 4, and a confession in verse 5. Then the problem resumes in verses 6-12, followed

by request in verses 13-18. Another statement of
the problem comes in verses 19-21, followed by
another request in 22-29. The profession of faith
does not come until verse 33, following the promise
to praise in verses 30-32. Then praise itself comes
in verses 34-36.

PSALM 69

For the leader; to the tune of *Lilies*; of David.

[1]Rescue me, O God; for the waters have
overcome my life.

[2]I drown in deep mire, where there is no
standing;
I have come into deep waters, where the floods
flounder me.

[3]I am weary with my weeping; my throat is
thirsty;
My eyes fail while I wait for my God.

[4]There are more that spurn me without cause
than there are hairs on my head;
Those that would cut me off, my enemies for
no reason, are mighty;
That which I did not steal, I have to restore.

[5]O God, you know my shameless behaviour;
and my disgraceful acts are not hidden from
you.

⁶Do not let those that wait for you be put to
shame through me, O LORD of Hosts;
Do not let those that seek you be brought to
dishonour through me, O God of Israel.

⁷Because for your sake I have borne blame;
shame has covered my face.

⁸I have become a stranger to my brothers and
an alien to my mother's sons.

⁹Because zeal for your house has consumed
me, and the insults of those that insult you
have fallen on me.

¹⁰When I wept and chastened my life with
fasting, I was insulted.

¹¹When I made sackcloth my clothing, I became
a farce to them.

¹²Those that sit in the gate talk of me; and
drunks sing about me.

¹³But as for me, my prayer is to you, O LORD,
in an acceptable time;
O God, in the abundance of your benevolence,
answer me in the truth of your rescue.

¹⁴Deliver me out of the dung, and do not let me
sink;
Let me be delivered from those that mock me
and out of the deep waters.

[15]Do not let the flood overwhelm me, nor the deep swallow me up;
And do not let the pit shut its mouth on me.

[16]Answer me, O LORD; for your benevolence is good;
According to your tender magnanimity, turn to me.

[17]And do not hide your face from your slave; for I am in distress; answer me speedily.

[18]Draw near to my life and ransom it; ransom me because of my enemies.

[19]You know my reproach, my shame, and my dishonour; My adversaries are all before you.

[20]Reproach has broken my heart and I am full of weariness;
And I looked for someone to take pity, but there was none;
And for comforters, but found none.

[21]They even gave me bile for my food; and in my thirst, they gave me vinegar to drink.

[22]Let their table before them become a trap; and for the secure ones, a snare.

[23]Let their eyes be darkened, so that they cannot see;
And make their loins continually to tremble.

[24]Pour out your indignation on them, and let the fierceness of your anger overtake them.

[25]Let their home be desolate; let none dwell in their tents.

[26]For they persecute him whom you have struck; and they tell of the sorrow of those whom you have wounded.

[27]Add iniquity to their iniquity; and do not let them come into your salvation.

[28]Let them be blotted out of the book of life, and not be written with the saved.

[29]But I am poor and sorrowful; Let your rescue, O God, set me up on high.

[30]I will praise the name of God with a song, and will magnify Him with recognition of my indebtedness.

[31]And it will please the LORD better than an ox or a bull that has horns and hoofs.

[32]The nonviolent have seen it, and are glad; You that seek after God, let your heart live.

[33]For the LORD hears the needy and does not ignore His prisoners.

[34]Let the heavens and earth praise Him, the seas, and everything that moves in it.

³⁵For God will rescue Zion, and rebuild the cities of Judah;
And they shall stay there, and have it in possession.

³⁶Even the descendants of His slaves shall inherit it; and those that give allegiance to His name shall dwell in it.

Psalm 13 is shorter and lacks one part. The appeal is verses 1-2, the problem and request are joined in verses 3-4, the avowal of innocence is missing, but the statement of trust is in verse 5. The promise to praise is in the first part of verse 6, in the future tense, while the last part of verse 7 is praise already, viewing God's action as already accomplished or underway.

PSALM 13

¹For the leader. A Psalm of David.

²How long, LORD? Will you utterly forget me?
How long will you hide your face from me?

³How long must I carry sorrow in my soul,
grief in my heart day after day?
How long will my foe triumph over me?

⁴Look upon me, answer me, LORD, my God!
Give light to my eyes lest I sleep in death,

⁵Lest my enemy say, "I have prevailed",
lest my foes revel in my downfall.

⁶But I trust in your faithfulness.
Grant my heart gladness in your help,
I will sing to the LORD,
For He has dealt bountifully with me!

You should be able, on your own, to identify the four parts of a thanksgiving in Psalm 30 and the seven stages of the lament for Psalm 17. In both cases, you may have to use a verse for more than one stage, and one or another of the stages may not appear.

PSALM 30

A Psalm. A song for the dedication of the Temple. Of David.

¹I praise you, LORD, for you picked me up
and did not let my enemies gloat over me.

²O LORD, my God,
I cried to you for help and you healed me.

³LORD, you brought my soul up from the tomb;
from going down to the pit,
you let me live.

⁴Sing praise to the LORD, you faithful;
give thanks to His holy memory.

⁵For His anger lasts but a moment;
His favour a lifetime.

At dusk, weeping comes for the night;
but at dawn, there is rejoicing.

[6]Complacent, I once said,
"I shall never be shaken".

[7]LORD, when you showed me favour
I stood like the mighty mountains.
But when you hid your face
I was hit with fear.

[8]To you, LORD, I cried out;
with the Lord, I pleaded for mercy.

[9]"What gain is there from my lifeblood,
from me going down to the grave?
Does dust give you thanks
or declare your constancy?

[10]Hear, O LORD, have mercy on me;
LORD, be my helper".

[11]You turned my tears into dancing;
you removed my sackcloth
and clothed me with gladness.

[12]So that my glory may praise you
and not be silent.
O LORD, my God,
forever will I give you thanks.

PSALM 17

A prayer of David.

[1]Hear, LORD, my plea for justice;
give heed to my cry;
Listen to my prayer
from lips without guile.

[2]Let my exoneration come from you;
For your eyes see what is right.

[3]You have tried my heart,
searched it in the night.
You have tried me by fire,
but find no malice in me.

[4]My lips have not offended
as mortals often do.
As I have learned from your lips,
I have guarded the way from the lawless.

[5]My steps have kept to your paths;
my feet have not faltered.

[6]I call upon you; answer me, O God.
Give ear to me; hear my appeal.

[7]Show your marvellous mercy,
you who save with your right arm
those who flee from their foes.

[8]Keep me as the apple of your eye;
shelter me in the shadow of your wings
from the wicked who rob me.

⁹My cruel foes press upon me;
they harden their hearts,
From their lips comes proud roaring.

¹⁰Their steps even now surround me;
they watch closely, crouched to the ground,

¹¹Like lions eager for prey,
like young lions poised to pounce.

¹²Rise up, O LORD, confront and cast them down;
save my soul from the wicked.

¹³Slay them with your sword;
with your hand, LORD, slay them;
snatch them from the world in their prime.

¹⁴Their bellies are being filled with your friends;
their children are stuffed too,
for they share what is left with their young.

¹⁵I am just—let me see your face;
when I awake, let me be filled with your presence.

WHY WERE THE PSALMS WRITTEN?

Form Criticism, which is what we have just gone through, is not an end in itself. There are many important things that we can learn from just dividing the Psalms into genres and from noting the parts of each genre, but most who practice Form Criticism hold that there is a relation between the exact form of writing and the social circumstance in which it is written. They want to go from an analysis of the form to a hypothesis about the occasion and purpose of composition. This can be used to better understand the Bible and biblical society.

There are allusions to temple service in the Psalms, as we saw in Chapter One. Were the Psalms as we have them written to be Temple hymns? Some scholars say, "No", the Psalms we have are based on earlier hymns, but are not the hymns themselves. Other scholars believe they are the hymns themselves, and some go so far as to identify specific Jewish feasts on which specific Psalms were used. So Psalms 24, 47, 95, 105, and 142 are said to be for the fall festival of Sukkoth or Booths. It is unlikely that we can be precise about which Psalms belong where, although certainly specific Psalms got assigned to specific feasts later in time, after the Book of Psalms had been around a while. Psalms 113-118 were used at Passover by the time of Jesus. A few scholars have argued that the Temple and synagogue were not the main use of the Psalms as much as they were for piety in the home.

An important question to begin with is why the Individual Laments are the largest group. Perhaps this is obvious. we are lamenting more in life than we are praising. Bad things happen, and we take them to God. If you look again at the format of the thanksgiving, you see that it is really a response to a lament. The lament predicts a thanksgiving, and the thanksgiving retells the crisis and salvation. Most other Psalm forms are derived from or responses to the lament.

Most laments are about one's enemies or sickness. You can divide sickness ones from enemy ones quite clearly - there are few mixes. If you list the fifteen sickness Psalms, there are only four mentions of enemies within them compared to forty-one mentions of sicknesses. There are twenty-five enemy Psalms, of which eleven concern false accusation (e.g., Psalms 7, 26, 27). One interpreter challenges us to ask, "Who is suffering this issue the most? Who listens to country music [our laments?] Who is sick more often?" In that sense, the Psalms are the songs of the poor.

FORM CRITICISM AND PSYCHOLOGY

The Psalms are about loss and happy surprise. The dominant ideology of our culture is committed to continuity and success and to the avoidance of pain, hurt, and loss. The dominant culture is also resistant to genuine newness and real surprise. It is curious but true, that surprise is as unwelcome as is loss. And our culture is organized to prevent the experience of both.

We have consigned lament to the therapist's office. The Psalms allow us to confront God with it. There is a close correspondence between the anatomy of the lament Psalm and the anatomy of the soul. Remember that anatomy is structurally central for all Psalms. Look again at the structure of the lament, and realize that this is God's inspired prayer for our lips. This is a pattern of prayer that God suggests to us as surely as He suggested the Lord's Prayer.

When we are angry with God, He wants to hear about it. There is nothing that cannot be said to Him in prayer. He knows we think He is not listening, so our prayer begins with a "Hear me!" Following this appeal, in the inspired pattern, we are to spell out the problem and then come out and ask for what we want. Some are too pious to ask, hiding behind theological statements that prayer does not change God, only us. Those statements have validity but the inspired models say, "Ask!" Often our real motive for not asking is a sinking feeling that He will not listen. Pay attention to element four, the avowal of innocence or confession of guilt. Now is the time for an examination of conscience. Then, and only then, God asks us to professes our trust in Him to save us. We do not start with the trust, but we do not pray without it. Sixth is a promise to thank God when saved, and seventh is actual praise of God.

Lament is complaining to God. We should not be too pious to practice it. Of course, for Christian faith, that characteristically Jewish embrace of and articulation of disorientation is decisively embodied in the Crucifixion of Jesus.

The parallel for the thanksgiving is the Resurrection. Here, too, our culture has consigned effusive praise to the sports arena. In both cases, as well as all the minor genres, we have more than model songs or prayers for our use. Praying in the style of the Psalms is great, but praying the Psalms is even better, as we shall see in the third chapter. Praying the Psalms changes us. St. Athanasius wrote "the distinctive nature of the Psalms lies in their ability to affect and mould a person" (*Letter to Marcellinus*, 13).

THE THEOLOGY OF THE BOOK OF PSALMS

The English Benedictine, Sebastian Moore, writes, "God behaves in the Psalms in ways He is not allowed to behave in systematic theology". It is useful for us to look at the theology of the Book of Psalms, and to do so first by asking who God is in the Psalms and then by asking who man is.

Who is God?

We can begin by looking at the portraits of God in the Psalms. This list is not meant to be in any order.

God is creator. That may seem rather obvious, but it is actually not a major theme in the Old Testament. Aside from Genesis, the fact that God is creator of all, especially of us, is not given much attention. The prophets rarely allude to it, and the wisdom literature does only to a slightly greater extent (in Job, for example). It is in the Psalms that we see much emphasis on this aspect of God's nature. Often God's power as creator is the source of confidence for the speaker in a lament (74:12-17). And quite often, it is God's creating that elicits praise in a hymn, as here in Psalm 19:

PSALM 19

For the leader. A Psalm of David.

¹The heavens declare the glory of God;
the sky proclaims the works of His hand.

²Day pours forth speech to day;
night whispers knowledge to night.

³Yet there is no speech, no words;
No voice is heard;

⁴A report goes forth through all the world,
the messages of the heavens, the sky, the day,
and the night, to the ends of the earth.
There, in them, He has pitched a tent for the
sun;

⁵Who comes forth like a bridegroom from his
canopy,
and like a hero joyfully running his course.

⁶From one end of the heavens it comes forth;
its course runs through to the other;
nothing escapes its heat.

⁷The precepts of the LORD are perfect,
refreshing the soul.
The teaching of the LORD is trustworthy,
educating the simple.

⁸The rulings of the LORD are right,
rejoicing the heart.
The command of the LORD is clear,
enlightening the eye.

⁹Reverence for the LORD is pure,
enduring forever.
The decrees of the LORD are true,
all of them just;

¹⁰More desirable than gold,
than a hoard of purest gold,
Sweeter even than honey
than drippings from the comb.

¹¹By them your servant is warned;
obeying them brings much reward.

¹²Who can see their own sins?
Cleanse me from my unseen errors.

¹³And hold your servant back from raging at
the haughty;
let my rage never control me.
Then I shall be blameless,
innocent of grave sin.

¹⁴Let the words of my mouth be acceptable,
the thoughts of my heart before you,
LORD, my rock and my redeemer.

God is also, however, intimately related to Israel.
He is the God of their history, and especially the
God of the Exodus (Psalm 81:5-11). In this, the
Psalms reflect similar theology to the prophets.
God is repeatedly described as a king (47:2; 74:12).
But specifically, He is a victorious warrior king
(24:7-10; 44:4). God is holy (29:2; 99:3-9), before
whom we tremble. But He is also merciful (25:6-
18). Could one pray a lament or a confession if He
were not? Moreover, praying a lament, and doing so
because God has revealed that we should, means
God is reliable (31:3-5). God is merciful, reliable,
and yet because He is holy, He is also an avenger of
injustice (34:7; 113:7-9)

In the Psalms, God is both present and remote,
both immanent and transcendent. Psalm 23, "the

Lord is my shepherd", speaks of God in very intimate terms, describing His nearness to us. Other Psalms talk about God dwelling with His people on Mt. Zion, in the Temple (132:13-16). At the same time, God is resplendent in unapproachable glory, infinitely transcendent (29; 93; 97:2).

PSALM 23

A Psalm of David.

¹The LORD is my shepherd;
there is nothing I lack.

²In green fields you pasture me;
by calm waters, you lead me;

³You restore my soul.
You guide me along paths of righteousness
for your name's sake.

⁴Even when I walk through a dark valley,
I fear no evil, for you are with me;
your rod and staff comfort me.

⁵You set a table before me
in front of my enemies;
You anoint my head with oil;
my cup overflows.

⁶Indeed, goodness and mercy will follow me
all the days of my life;
I will dwell in the house of the LORD
for endless days.

Who is Man?

Who is man in the Book of Psalms? Again, it is a varied picture, a complete picture. Man has incredible dignity. Psalm 8:3-8 makes him little less than the angels, given dominion over all God's creation and worthy of God's attention. Psalm 103:14-16, on the other hand, presents man's transitory existence, likening us to dust and passing flowers.

Do the Psalms contain a picture of the afterlife? It is important to remember that the Psalms come from many different periods. Early in Israel's history, they did not yet understand the nature of eternal life and believed all men went to a shadowy realm called Sheol, where nothing happened. Only later did an understanding of eternal life, final judgment, and resurrection emerge, and even then, it was not accepted by many in Judaism, the Sadducees, for instance. Many of the Psalms build on an early understanding of Sheol (88:35, 10-12). In fact, some laments almost come to the point of trying to bribe God by telling Him that quite obviously, no one can praise Him from Sheol, and so wouldn't it be better for Him to save them? Nevertheless, in a few Psalms we see the emerging understanding that there is more. Psalm 49:15 says, "God will ransom my soul from the power of Sheol, for He will receive me". This is incipient hope in a life with God after death.

CONCLUSION

We have seen how easy it is to divide the Book of Psalms into various genres, particularly into individual and collective hymns, thanksgivings and laments. You have learned the structure or components of those major types of Psalms, which are really models for prayer. Finally, we looked at the portrait of God and man that the Book of Psalms contributes to biblical theology.

FOR FURTHER STUDY

By way of a practical application of this chapter, let us try some of the following when next prayerfully reading the Psalms:

Identify the genre of a Psalm. This allows you to not mistake the confidence in a lament for a happy Psalm or the description of crisis in a thanksgiving for a lament, and that will help you "stay with the tone" or mood of the Psalm you are praying.

Identify the components of the Psalm you are reading. Let them guide you through a spiritual process from one component to the next.

Chapter Three

The Psalms as the Quintessential Prayers for Today

THE PSALMS IN THE NEW TESTAMENT

There are fifty-five citations of the Psalms in the New Testament. That amounts to a third of all the quotations from the Old Testament in the New. A point of trivia is that the first person in the New Testament to quote the Psalms is the devil! In Matt 4:6, he quotes Psalm 91.

Jesus used verses from the Psalms to challenge the leaders in Jerusalem to recognize His true identity. He quotes Psalm 110:1, "The Lord's revelation to my Lord, 'Sit on my right: your foes I will put beneath your feet'" to show that the Messiah is greater than David (Luke 20:41-44). His triumphal entry into Jerusalem on Palm Sunday recalled Psalm 118:26-27, "Blessed is he who comes in the name of the Lord. We bless you from the house of the Lord; the Lord God is our light. Go forwards in procession with branches even to the altar". And at the Cross, He cried out in the words of Psalm 22:1, "My God, my God, why have you forsaken me?" Citations in Acts show that Psalms came to the minds and lips of earliest Christians readily. St. Peter uses Psalms 16 and 110 to convince the crowd of Jesus' resurrection (Acts 2:24-29). St. Paul uses Psalms 2, 16, and 89 when preaching in Pisidian Antioch (Acts 13:32-37). The Letter to the Hebrews uses Psalms more than any other New Testament book, quoting eleven different Psalms. Hebrews 1:5-14 rattles off quotations from Psalms 2, 97, 104, 102, and 110 in a Scriptural proof that Christ is greater than the angels.

PSALM 16

A *miktam* of David.

¹Keep me safe, O God;
in you, I take refuge.

²I say to the LORD,
you are my Lord,
you are my only good.

³And the holy ones of the land,
they are made grand,
all my delight is in them.

⁴But they feed their trials
who court other gods.
I will not pour out blood libations to them,
nor take their names upon my lips.

⁵LORD, my appointed portion and my cup,
you have made my destiny secure.

⁶Pleasant places were measured out for me;
fair to me indeed is my inheritance.

⁷I bless the LORD who counsels me;
even at night, my heart exhorts me.

⁸I keep the LORD always before me;
with Him at my right, nothing alarms me.

⁹Therefore my heart is glad, my soul rejoices;
my body dwells secure.

¹⁰For you will not abandon my soul to the grave,
nor your devoted one to the pit.

¹¹You will point me to the path to life,
plentiful joy in your presence,
delight at your right hand forever.

In general, the New Testament authors apply the Psalms directly and immediately to their own stories in order to instruct or edify. The way in which they do this is called *Midrash*. Midrash aims to penetrate into the Scripture's inner significance and is often homiletic. The pieces of interpretation are intended to make the biblical text refer to the history and circumstances of the early Christian community within which the writings of the New Testament were composed.

THE EARLY CHURCH AND THE PSALMS

In the early Church, it seems average Christians had the Psalms memorized. Clement of Alexandria says farmers and boatmen sing them; Theodore of Mopsuestia says you hear them in the markets; St. Jerome says he heard them sung in gardens. They are always the dying words of the martyrs (e.g., St. Crispin, St. Maurice). And the Church Fathers, early writers of the Church before 750 AD, comment more on the Psalms than on any other book of the Bible, including the New Testament books.

When it comes to the Psalms, the Church Fathers gave primarily Midrash interpretation. They were interested in the meaning expressed by the texts when read, under the influence of the Holy Spirit, in the context of the paschal mystery of Christ and of the new life that flows from it. Thus, St. Justin Martyr (ca. 100-165 AD), in His *Dialogue with Trypho*, interprets Psalms 22 and 110 and the Royal Psalms (see Chapter Two) as referring to Jesus.

St. Hilary

St. Hilary (315-367) likewise interprets the Psalms as referring to Christ, or more precisely, as being prophetically the words of Christ. In His *Homily* on Psalm 1, he writes, "In what we might call the majority of Psalms, the Person of the Son is introduced, as in the seventeenth [our Psalm 18, see Chapter One]: A people whom I have not known hath served Me [verse 45]". Moreover, the voice of Christ alternates with voice of Church (e.g., in Psalms 124-125). His interpretations are not always "Christological", but may be what might be called the Moral Sense, applicable to our daily lives. So, again in His homily on Psalm 1, he says of verse 1, "The man who has not walked in the counsel of the ungodly shall not stand in the way of sinners. For there are many whose confession concerning God, while it acquits them of ungodliness, yet does not set them free from sin; those, for example, who abide in the Church but do not observe her laws". He will also sometimes read texts as spiritual, mystical representations of future or heavenly realities. In a homily on Psalm 131, verse 2 "Like a weaned child upon His mother's breast, so will thou reward my soul", he writes that the Psalmist "prays that God, because he has not lifted up His heart, nor walked amid things great and wonderful that are above him, because he has not been humble-minded but did lift up His soul, may reward His soul, lying like a weaned child upon His mother; that is to say that he may be deemed worthy of the reward of the perfect, heavenly and living bread".

PSALM 131

[1]A song of ascents. Of David.
LORD, my heart is not haughty;
nor are my eyes arrogant.
I do not busy myself with world politics,
with things beyond me.

[2]Rather, I have stilled my soul,
Like a weaned child hushed at its mother,
Like a hushed child is my soul.

[3]Israel, hope in the LORD,
now and forever.

In all of these senses, however, St. Hilary grounds His interpretation in the text itself, in the plain sense of its meaning. These spiritual meanings are in continuity with the literal meaning, just on a different level.

St. Athanasius

St. Athanasius (295-373), Patriarch of Alexandria in Egypt, wrote a *Letter to Marcellinus on Interpretation of Psalms*. If you are interested, you can read this letter yourself at http://www.athanasius.com/psalms/aletterm.htm. Because he was writing to an individual Christian about how to read the Psalms, St. Athanasius is more personal than St. Hilary. Many of his insights we will return to when we discuss how we might pray the Psalms.

St. Athanasius separated the Psalms out into genres, much as we did in Chapter Two. He separates thanksgiving, confessions, and so forth. He then says that, knowing the mood of a given Psalm, the Christian can recite these prayers as though they were His own. Doing so will actually change you. He wrote, "The distinctive nature of the Psalms lies in their ability to affect and mould a person".

St. Basil

Another Church Father who worked with Form Criticism was St. Basil the Great (329-379), from what is now Turkey. St. Basil spent less time on the genres, however, and gave more attention to the "format" of the Psalms. Recall the components of Psalms of thanksgiving or lament that we examined in Chapter Two. St. Basil likewise found these components, and he noted parallelism, as well (see Chapter One). Both Sts. Athanasius and Basil continued to interpret the Psalms also through Midrash. On Psalm 87:2, St. Athanasius wrote, "'The Lord loves the gates of Zion more than all the tabernacles of Jacob.' 'Gates of Zion' means the introductory and elementary teaching of the Church; while 'tabernacles of Jacob' refers to the worship in accordance with the Law. It means, then, that the polity of the Gospel has been judged by God to be preferable to the worship according to the Law". Nevertheless, they did not do more than find a "spiritual sense" for the words of the Psalm.

PSALM 87

A Psalm of the Korahites. A song.

[1]Its foundations are on holy mountains:

[2]The LORD loves the gates of Zion
more than any settlement in Jacob.

[3]Glorious things are said of you,
O city of God!
Selah

[4]Rahab and Babylon I count
Among those who know me.
See, of Philistia and Tyre, with Ethiopia, I say,
"This one was born there".

[5]And of Zion, it will be said:
"*Each one* was born in it".
The Most High will establish this;

[6]The Lord notes in the register of the peoples;
"This one, too, was born there".
Selah

[7]So say singers and dancers;
"All my springs are in you".

St. Ambrose

Things began to change, however, with St. Ambrose of Milan (338-397), in Italy. He wrote a *Commentary on Twelve Psalms*, and began by using Form Criticism. He followed it through all the way to suggesting a historical setting for the Psalm's composition. Unfortunately, many of these settings originated in his imagination. The supposed historical settings St. Ambrose then interpreted allegorically or symbolically, especially about Christ. This was different from the earlier allegorical interpretations of the *words* of the Psalms.

St. Augustine

These trends were continued by his student, St. Augustine (354-430). St. Augustine, in his *Expositions of the Psalms*, understood the Psalm titles, for example, not to refer to events in David's life but to be prophetic about Christ. Most everything was understood Christologically: Psalm 1, "'Blessed is the man that hath not gone away in the counsel of the ungodly' (ver. 1). This is to be understood of our Lord Jesus Christ, the Lord Man". In fact, the titles especially held mysteries. St. Augustine wrote that "Asaph" "in Hebrew means synagogue" (he was wrong about that) and so stands for the Jews (as in Psalm 74).

St. Jerome

Likewise, St. Jerome (343-420), whose *Tractates on the Psalms* would be used alongside Augustine's *Expositions* as the standard texts on the Psalms for the Middle Ages, was largely occupied with allegory and prophecy. He condemned those supporters of the literal sense who neglected deeper spiritual meanings. St. Jerome also interpreted the titles symbolically. Asaph now meant, "Gathering with the Lord", and "Korah" referred to Calvary.

This kind of symbolic interpretation was dominant in the Church until St. Thomas Aquinas in the late 1200s again taught that since the end purpose of this Scripture is prayer, which is the raising of the mind to God, the Psalms "teach how to praise God with exultation". Still, if Ambrose, Augustine, and Jerome are laid to one side, we shall see that the Church Fathers' commentary on the Book of Psalms has much relevance to our own praying of the Psalms.

PRAYING AND SINGING THE PSALMS

First, we might ask why one would pray the Psalms. The answer is that just as we learn to write by copying the shape of the letters, so we learn to pray by copying the inspired prayers that the Book of Psalms gives us to suit every need. Using these inspired examples counters any potential dangers of complete free-form prayer. Praying the Book of Psalms teaches us the proper balance of penance, festivity, contrition, praise, petition, and thanks. St. Athanasius wanted the Psalms to be widely prayed to counter "the heretics who seduced people with hymns and prayers that gratified their religious sentiments".

The Jewish Horarium

Praying the Psalms is also a very old tradition of the Church, especially praying the Psalms at certain hours of the day in order to sanctify the day. Jews at the time of Christ prayed at specific hours of the day and usually with Psalms. They prayed at three set hours: morning, afternoon, and evening. Peter and John are going to join the afternoon prayers in Acts 3:1. The Jewish "office" of prayer was not uniform by the time Christians and Jews parted ways, and so there is likely no *direct* continuity with the Christian "Liturgy of the Hours" (also known as the Divine Office). But, morning and evening prayer were the most general and privileged hours of prayer in all traditions of early Judaism, just as they would become in Christianity. In Acts 10:3, 9, and 30, we see that Jews and Christians still maintained the same prayer schedule at least regarding the afternoon prayer.

The History of Praying the Psalms

The earliest record of prayer at set times is in the first letter of St. Clement of Rome (*1 Clement* 40:1-4), from the late 1st century AD. He says that prayer at set times was the norm for all Christians.

The first solid evidence for what those set times were is from Clement of Alexandria about a hundred years later. He records that Christians prayed at 6:00 am, 9:00 am, noon, 3:00 pm, 6:00 pm, and once during the night. You may already know that these are the same "hours" of prayer that are used in the Episcopal and Catholic Churches today. They used to go by the names, "Lauds, Terce, Sext, None, Vespers, and Vigil". At about the same time, St. Hippolytus of Rome and another Christian writer named Tertullian indicate that all Christians were obliged to pray Morning and Evening and that the other four were highly recommended. We will return to this idea that even the laity was included in these prayers.

It is not possible, however, to say that it was the Psalms being prayed at these hours. The first we can be sure it's Psalms is in the early 300s. By then, the obligation of the prayers was only for monks, although as late as the 800s, large congregations of lay people would gather at the monasteries to join in what was coming to be called the "Divine Office".

The actual form of the Divine Office, or praying of the Psalms at the set hours, looked remarkably like what it does today in the Catholic and Episcopal traditions. (We will look at the format of today's later). St. John Cassian records in 415 that the custom was the same among monks in Egypt, Palestine,

Iraq, and France. He reports that the Psalms were sung. That was the nature of their origin, as we saw in Chapter One, and was the norm for their praying for most of Christian history. At the end of each Psalm, the Gloria was prayed, just as it is today. Antiphons were added to the Psalms, again just as today.

A schema to pray the whole Book of Psalms in one week was in place in all monastic communities by the 600s with the Rule of St. Benedict. The set hours of prayer were the same as before, the same as we have today. The Hebrew titles were not prayed, but new titles were introduced that usually emphasize the interpretation of the Psalm as the voice of Christ. These titles went out of use in the 1200s, but were re-introduced in the 1700s and are in the current Catholic "Liturgy of the Hours". Prayers were added after the period of silence that follows each Psalm, prayers that conclude the Psalm's sentiments. Today these are called "Psalm-prayers". The Psalms were still always sung. Where earlier soloists had sometimes been used, the practice of alternating between two halves of the group present, verse by verse, was brought to Europe from Syria by St. Ambrose in 386. That is still how the Liturgy of the Hours is usually prayed. Also, by 600 the choice of texts was almost the same as it has been to this day -- Psalms 140-141 is central for Evening Prayer, 63 for Morning.

Beginning in the 800s, the Church extended the requirement of praying all the hours to all priests, not just monks. Meanwhile, in the monasteries, private recitation was emerging — the first references to it are from St. Peter Damian (d. 1072). But the first big step towards saying the Divine Office in private instead of in a group came with the Franciscans (ca. 1300), the first order to not be tied to one place. Because the Franciscans "wandered" about, it was necessary to recite the Office in private wherever they happened to be. This also marked the beginning of "saying" the Psalms instead of singing them; if you were praying alone you were less likely to sing aloud! Additionally, the Pope and His assistants had lots of work to do and so had shortened the Office to a portable book called a "breviary". That suited the wandering Franciscans well, and so they adopted it and then spread it across Western Christendom.

For a long time, the Church continued to say that celebrating the Office together was better, but by 1400, it had become the norm. This was related to a turn from public, communal devotion to personal piety of the interior life. The decisive influence in the Catholic Church was the Jesuits — they had no obligation or even preference for choral recitation, and no founder of a religious order in history more resolutely refused to make any legislation whatever concerning the prayer of his formed religious than Ignatius of Loyola. Most religious orders formed thereafter were in their image, and the Jesuits renewed the Catholic Church after the Reformation. The Psalms became something priests and monks prayed, usually in private, without singing.

By the 20th century, the hours had migrated around the clock in the Catholic Church. The original Morning Prayer, Lauds, had moved earlier into the night, necessitating the introduction of "Prime" at 6:00 am. Evening Prayer or Vigil had into the middle of the night and become "Matins", literally morning. So priests got up twice in the night, to pray Matins and Lauds. "Compline" was added where Vigil had been.

The Catholic Church's Second Vatican Council mandated the restructuring of the Divine Office in its 1963 *Constitution on the Liturgy (Sacrosanctum Concilium)*. It mandated that the prayers should return to their hours; Lauds moved from pre-dawn to Morning (renamed Morning Prayer), Vespers stayed as the Evening Prayer and Compline as Night Prayer. Prime was eliminated, and priests who were not monks were required to only pray one of Terce, Sext, or None as their "Daytime Prayer". Matins became an hour of prayer for any time in day, known now as the Office of Readings. A new "Breviary" for the Liturgy of the Hours was called for. Pope Paul VI in 1970 promulgated a new Liturgy of the Hours and in 1974, it appeared in English translation. In 1976, a one-volume edition appeared with the title *Christian Prayer*. It is particularly suited for praying by the laity.

The Role of Lay People

But why would lay people want to pray the Liturgy of the Hours? We have already shown why you should pray the Psalms. It is also a part of Christian tradition that the Liturgy of the Hours is the prayer of all the members of the Church. The *Lutheran Book of Worship* includes the Psalms and instructions for their singing, as do *Evangelical Lutheran Worship* published by the Evangelical Lutheran Church in America and the *Lutheran Service Book* of the Lutheran Church-Missouri Synod.

EARLY CHURCH

In the early Church, St. Hippolytus said around 200 AD that lay people prayed the Divine Office. The Book of Psalms has been uniquely available to laity throughout history – for a long time it was only thing a layperson could read out in Church.

Characteristics of the Divine Office

It is beyond the theme of this chapter to describe the Catholic Liturgy of the Hours or Anglican *Common Worship: Daily Prayer* in detail, and to be honest it is impossible to explain how it is done without having it in front of you. But we can look at some of its characteristics.

The Liturgy of the Hours is designed so that the entire Book of Psalms can be prayed in four weeks. Titles, Psalm-Prayers, and Antiphons have been added to the Psalms to aid in understanding, and these are all very ancient additions, as we have seen. There is always a Scripture reading, other than a Psalm, and an optional responsorial Psalm. Other parts of the Office and the cycles and calendars by which it operates, requires looking at the Liturgy of the Hours itself, but it is not difficult and one should not hesitate to do so.

Singing is the preferred way of praying the Psalms. We have seen that this was the traditional way of praying the Office. It is also preferred that the Office be prayed in a group, as was the early tradition.

The only Psalms the Liturgy of the Hours omits are 58, 83, 105, 106, and 109. These are, for the most part, cursing Psalms. Could they fruitfully be prayed? I am not sure. Should we curse our enemies? Perhaps that is the wrong question to ask, since we often already do in our hearts. All of the curses are found in laments, like the example from Chapter One of the Babylonian babies. This gives voice to our hearts and we are purged, cleansed. Denial of pain does not make it go away, nor does taking revenge on our own. Healing comes only with bringing it to God. The Psalms defeat our tendency to try to be holy without being human first.

The Role of Form Criticism

When we pray the Psalms, we must focus on plain, literal sense. An understanding of the literal meaning of the Psalms helps to relate the text to the believer's daily life. The Psalms express the gamut of human emotions. Columba Marmion said, "There is no inward disposition of our souls that they cannot express", and Pope John Paul II said, "In the Psalms, the human being fully discovers himself". That means the words of the Psalm we pray can really become our prayers. St. Athanasius wrote to Marcellinus, "The Psalms as I view them are like a mirror in which the reader can see himself and the movements of His soul; he can recite these prayers as though this were actually so". St. John Cassian says the Christian reads "as if he himself were the author, and as a personal prayer".

It is precisely here that Form Criticism is such a great help. We can use Form Criticism to find quickly the genre of a given Psalm, and then open our hearts to the attitudes it expresses via its format. And vice-versa, we can find a Psalm that fits the prayer need we have at a given moment by using Form Criticism to identify the genres. Praying the appropriate Psalm in that case will shape our own prayer.

Praying in the Name of the Church, In the Person of Christ

PRAYING IN THE NAME OF THE CHURCH

As important as this is, and as fruitful as it can be for our prayer life, it is not enough. We cannot simply use Form Criticism to find a Psalm that speaks to where we are at and then pray it. That is not enough, because we pray the Psalms "in the name of the Church". The Divine Office is not a private matter. We should pray *all* the Psalms, and it does not matter if they express adequately what we feel at a given moment. The great Lutheran theologian Dietrich Bonheoffer said that if it depended on that, all we would pray is "Give us this day our daily bread".

Notice how many prayers we classified as Collective/Communal in Chapter Two. The plural prayer is an old Jewish tradition; we are always praying for others with us. Thomas Merton said that if we only arrive at personal fulfilment in Christ, we fall far short of the contemplation the Book of Psalms has in store.

If you pray the Liturgy of the Hours, quite often the emotions expressed are not yours at the time. This is so that the intentions and needs of the Universal Church would be remembered in community prayer. Experientially, in terms of faith situation, the personal and public issues are all of a piece (cf. Romans 12:15). And this, too, is moulding your prayer and teaching you. John Paul II said, "By praying the Psalms as a community, the Christian mind remembered and understood that it is impossible to turn to the Father who dwells in heaven without an authentic communion of life with one's brothers and sisters who live on earth". This also speaks to the need to pray it in common, not only priests with other priests but parish groups and families together.

PRAYING IN THE PERSON OF CHRIST

We are also supposed to pray the Psalms "in the person of Christ". This will take some unpacking. Dietrich Bonheoffer says, "If we want to read and to pray the Psalms, we must not ask first what they have to do with us, but what they have to do with Jesus Christ". We have already seen how the Church Fathers more and more put the words of the Psalms into the mouth of Christ. St. Augustine was clear that this did not exclude the Psalms being the words of the Church; he wrote, "either of the voice of Christ alone or the voice of the Church alone because in part we form the same body". John Paul II, too, said that it is always Christ who speaks in the Psalms, "but the *Christus totus,* the total Christ, composed of Christ the Head and His members". In the use of the Psalms, we are moving back and forth among the reference to Jesus, the voice of the Psalm itself, and our own and the Church's experiences.

But is that all "praying in the person of Christ" means? Thomas Merton says, "When a Christian chants the Office, then he not only understands the Psalms, but he fulfils them". In the Holy Spirit, through His Church, Christ carries on His work of the sanctification of men and the praise of God not only when the Eucharist is celebrated and the sacraments administered, but also, in addition to other ways, when the Liturgy of the Hours is prayed. Our praying of the Psalms, particularly in the Liturgy of the Hours, is an exercise of Christ's priestly office. What an immense privilege! The question is not, then, "Why pray the Liturgy of the Hours?" but "Why not accept this tremendous mission?" But we are not sanctifying the world, Christ is. As members of the body of Christ, our worldwide chorus of biblical prayer is actually an expression of the heart of the risen Son of God sitting at the right hand of the Father. To be allowed to join in with His prayer is a mysterious privilege understandable only through faith.

CONCLUSION

We have seen that the Psalms have always been the Prayer of the Church, not only for clergy but for laity as well. The churches strongly encourage you to pray the Psalms. Form Criticism can open up the Psalms for you as personal prayer, but we are called to much more than that, as we pray in the name of the Church in the person of Christ.

FOR FURTHER STUDY

By way of a practical application of this chapter, let us try some of the following when next prayerfully reading the Psalms.

Imagine the words of the Psalm you are reading as coming from the mouth of Christ. This may be easiest with the Individual and Royal Psalms.

Use what you learned in Chapter Two of Form Criticism to find a Psalm that does *not* fit where you are currently in your spiritual life, and then pray that Psalm on behalf of an unknown member of the Church who *is*.

Find a copy of the one-volume Catholic Liturgy of the Hours entitled *Christian Prayer* or the Episcopal *Contemporary Office Book* or *St. Helena Breviary* and have at it!

Index

A

Accents, 5
Acrostics, 18, 20
Acts, 78, 87
Afterlife, 75
Alexandria, 34, 80, 82, 88
Allegory, 85-86
Ambrose, 84-86, 89
Anglican Church, 6, 92
Antiphons, 89, 93
Antithetic Parallelism, 7
Asaph, 24-25, 85-86
Ascents, Songs of, 27
Athanasius, 34, 70,
    82-83, 86, 94
Augustine, 85-86, 96
Authors, 23, 79

B

Babylon, 13-15, 84, 93
Basil, 83
Benedict, 89
Benedictines, 70
Bernard, 21
Blessings, 43, 46, 49
Bonheoffer, Dietrich,
    95-96
Breviary, 91, 98

C

Choirmaster, 27
Christ, 19-20, 78, 80-81,
    85, 87, 89, 95-98
Christological, 81, 85
Chronicles, 23, 25
Clement, 80, 87-88
Collective, 34-35, 37, 44,
    50, 76, 95
Compline, 91
Confessions, 57, 69, 73,
    81, 83
Confidence, Psalms of, 50
Congregations, 88
Crispin, 80
Curses, 54, 93

D

David, 23-25, 42-43,
    47-49, 62-63, 65, 77-78
Dead Sea Scrolls, 19, 22,
    29
Death, 9, 38, 55-56, 62,
    75
Doxologies, 29

E

Egypt, 16, 19, 82, 89

Enemies, 36, 38-39, 41-43, 58, 60, 62-63
Ethan, 25
Evening Prayer, 88-89, 91
Exodus, 73

F
Form Criticism, 33, 66, 83-84, 94-95, 98
Franciscans, 90

G
Genre, 5-6, 33-34, 44-45, 53-54, 66, 70, 76, 83, 94
Gittith, 46
Gloria, 89
Gradual Psalms, 27
Greek, 2, 19, 26
Gregory of Nyssa, 28

H
Hallelujah, 2, 4, 56
Harp, 13, 28
Hebrews, Letter to the, 78
Heman, 25
Hilary of Poitiers, 34, 80, 82
Hippolytus, 29, 88, 92
Historical Psalms, 73, 75, 79, 85, 87, 89-90, 92
Hours, Liturgy of the, 87, 89, 91-93, 95, 97-98
Hymns, 5-6, 34, 36, 54

I
Individual, 25, 34-36, 44-45

Instruments, 2, 26-28
Israel, 8, 10, 16-17, 73, 75

J
Jacob, 10, 12, 46, 50-51, 83-84
Jerome, 19, 21, 29, 80, 85-86
Jerusalem, 14-15, 18, 23, 26-27, 47-48,
Jesuits, 90-91
Jesus, 67, 70, 77-78, 80, 85, 96-97
Job, 52, 71
John Cassian, 88, 94
Judaism, 19, 75, 85, 87

K
King, 12, 17, 34, 37, 42-44, 46, 50, 73
Kinnor, 28
Korah, Sons of, 24-25, 30, 46, 50, 84, 86

L
Laity, 88, 92, 98
Laments, 5, 26, 34-35, 44-45, 57, 63, 67-71, 73, 75-76, 83, 93
Lauds, 88, 91
Levites, 24
Lilies, 27, 58
Lowth, Robert, 6
Lutheran Church, 92, 95

M
Marmion, Columba, 94

Martyrs, 80
Maskil, 26
Matins, 91
Maurice, 80
Merton, Thomas, 95, 97
Meter, 3, 5-6
Midrash, 79-80, 83
Miktam, 26, 78
Mizmor, 26
Monasteries, 88, 90-91
Morning Prayer, 88-89, 91
Moses, 24-25

N

Nations, 4, 11, 42, 51
Numbering of the
    Psalms, 20-22

O

Office, Divine, 69, 87-88,
    90-95, 97-98

P

Parallelism, 6-7, 13-15,
    30, 83
Paul, 78, 91, 94, 96
Pentateuch, 1, 30
Peter, 78, 87
Peter Damian, 90
Petition, 57, 86
Pilgrimage, 27, 45-46
Poetry, 2-3, 6, 13, 30
Praise, 4, 10, 35-37,
    42, 44, 54-55, 57-58,
    61-64, 69-71
Prayer, 2, 12, 23, 25, 31,
    45-46, 59, 65, 69-70,

76-77, 83, 86-92,
    94-96, 97-98
Priests, 90-91, 96
Prime, 91
Proverbs, 1, 52
Psalm-Prayers, 93

R

Resurrection, 70, 75, 78
Rhythm, 3, 5-6
Royal Psalms, 34-35, 37,
    44

S

Sebastian, 70
Selah, 12, 27, 43, 46,
    50-51, 84
Septuagint, 18, 20-22, 24,
    26-27
Sext, 88, 91
Sheol, 37, 38, 55, 64, 73,
    75, 79
Shepherd, 21, 50, 74
Shiggaion, 26
Solomon, 25
Sopranos, 27, 50
Stich(s), 3-7, 13, 18
Strings, 28
Sukkoth, 67
Syllables, 5
Synagogue, 67, 85
Syriac, 19

T

Temple, 23, 25-26, 36,
    38, 48, 63, 67, 74
Terce, 88, 91

Tertullian, 88
Thanksgiving, 34-37,
   44-45, 47, 54-57,
   63-64, 68, 70, 76, 83,
   86
Theodore of
   Mopsuestia, 80
Thomas Aquinas, 86
Title(s), 8, 21-27, 29-30,
   35, 85-86, 89, 92-93

V
Vespers, 88, 91
Vigils, 88, 91
Vulgate, 19, 21

W
Wisdom, 1, 52, 71

Z
Zion, 12-14, 46, 62, 74,
   83-84